McGraw-Hill Reading
WonderWo...

Unit 7
Decodable Reader

Mc
Graw
Hill
Education

Bothell, WA • Chicago, IL • Columbus, OH • New York, NY

Contents

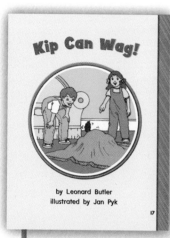

by Leonard Butler
illustrated by Jan Pyk

17

Deb Can Kick It!

by Frances Glennon
illustrated by Meryl Henderson

We **are** fit.
We can kick.

Deb is ten.
She **is** a Jet.

Deb can go.
Bam, Deb can kick it!

Deb ran, ran, ran.
Deb can not let Kim kick it!

Deb can kick it in the net.
It did not hit the rim.

Deb led.
Deb **was** on top!

Fun in the Sun

by Helen Lee

illustrated by Anni Matsick

Bud can run up to Pat.
Pat can pet Bud.

Lad can run up to Pat.
Pat can pet Lad.

Bud can nap and nap.
Lad can lap it up.

Bud and Lad can run **for** fun.
Bud and Lad can dip in.

Mom and Dad **have** fun.
Pat and Bud **have** fun.

It is fun in the sun!

Kip Can Wag!

by Leonard Butler

illustrated by Jan Pyk

Meg and Gus can see Kip.
Kip is on top **of** the big rug.

Did Kip run?

They can not see Kip!

Kip is not on the big rug.
Gus can pat it.

Kip got in the rug!
Kip hid in it!

The rug can wag!
It is Kip in the rug.

Meg can hug Kip.
Gus can pet Kip.
Kip can wag!

Unit 7

Decodable Words

Target Phonics Elements: Review Short *e*;
Consonants /f/f, /r/r; Final /b/b; Consonant /l/l; Initial
/h/ h, /k/k; Digraph *ck*
bam, Deb, fit, hit, kick, Kim, led, let, pack, rim
Review: *can, did, it, net, not, on, top*

High-Frequency Words
are, is, she, was
Review: *a, go, the*

Decodable Words

Target Phonics Element: Short *u*
Bud, fun, run, sun, up
Review: *can, Dad, dip, in, it, Lad, lap, Mom, nap,
Pat, pet*

High-Frequency Words
for, have
Review: *and, is, the, to*

Decodable Words

Target Phonics Elements: Initial and Final /g/*g*,
Consonant /w/*w*
big, got, Gus, hug, Meg, rug, wag
Review: *can, did, hid, in, it, Kip, not, on, pat, pet, run, top*

High-Frequency Words

of, they
Review: *and, is, see, the*

Decoding skills taught to date:

Consonants /m/*m,* /s/*s,* /p/*p,* /t/*t;* Short *a;* Short *i;* Initial and Final /n/*n;* Initial /k/*c;* Short *o;* Initial and Final /d/*d;* Consonant /h/*h;* Short *e;* Consonants /f/*f,* /r/*r;* Initial and Final /b/*b;* Consonant /l/*l;* Initial /k/*k;* Digraph *ck;* Short *u;* Initial and Final /g/*g;* Consonant /w/*w*